Collins easy learning

Times tables

Ages 7–11

Simon Greaves
Helen Greaves

How to use this book

- Find a quiet, comfortable place to work, away from other distractions.
- Help with reading the instructions where necessary and ensure that your child understands what they are required to do.
- Help and encourage your child to check their own answers as they complete each activity.
- Discuss with your child what they have learnt.
- Let your child return to their favourite pages once they have been completed, to talk about the activities.
- Reward your child with plenty of praise and encouragement.

Special features

- Yellow boxes: Introduce and outline the key times tables ideas.
- Did you know …? boxes: Give handy hints to help understanding of the key times tables ideas.

Published by Collins
An imprint of HarperCollins*Publishers*
1 London Bridge Street
London SE1 9GF

Browse the complete Collins catalogue at collins.co.uk

© HarperCollins*Publishers* 2008
This edition © HarperCollins*Publishers* 2015

12

ISBN 978-0-00-813440-2

Printed in Great Britain by
Bell and Bain Ltd, Glasgow

The authors assert their moral rights to be identified as the authors of this work.

British Library Cataloguing in Publication Data
A Catalogue record for this publication is available from the British Library

Written by Simon Greaves and Helen Greaves
Design by Graham M Brasnett and Jouve
Illustrated by Graham Smith
Cover design by Sarah Duxbury and Paul Oates
Cover illustration by John Haslam
Project managed by Sonia Dawkins

Contents

Three times table

The three times table tells you how to count in sets of three.

Read the three times table out loud.

$1 \times 3 = 3$

$2 \times 3 = 6$

$3 \times 3 = 9$

$4 \times 3 = 12$

$5 \times 3 = 15$

$6 \times 3 = 18$

$7 \times 3 = 21$

$8 \times 3 = 24$

$9 \times 3 = 27$

$10 \times 3 = 30$

$11 \times 3 = 33$

$12 \times 3 = 36$

Now fill in these answers.

$5 \times 3 = \boxed{}$

$\boxed{} \times 3 = 3$

$7 \times \boxed{} = 21$

$\boxed{} \times 3 = 33$

$3 \times 3 = \boxed{}$

$\boxed{} \times 3 = 18$

$10 \times \boxed{} = 30$

$12 \times 3 = \boxed{}$

$\boxed{} \times 3 = 27$

$4 \times \boxed{} = 12$

$8 \times 3 = \boxed{}$

$2 \times \boxed{} = 6$

Did you know ... ?

To triple a number means to multiply it by three.

1 Find a path through the maze. You can only pass through numbers that are in the three times table.

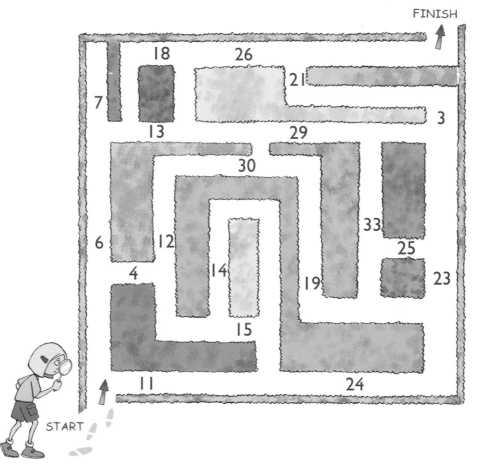

FINISH

18   26
      21
7
13   29
   30
        33
6   12   25
4   14   23
   19
   15
11   24

START

2 Every number put into the number machine is multiplied by three.

Fill in the missing numbers.

×3

☐ → → → → 9

☐ → → → → 24

☐ → → → → 3

☐ → → → → 18

Four times table

Read the four times table out loud.

$1 \times 4 = 4$

$2 \times 4 = 8$

$3 \times 4 = 12$

$4 \times 4 = 16$

$5 \times 4 = 20$

$6 \times 4 = 24$

$7 \times 4 = 28$

$8 \times 4 = 32$

$9 \times 4 = 36$

$10 \times 4 = 40$

$11 \times 4 = 44$

$12 \times 4 = 48$

Now fill in these answers.

$10 \times 4 = \boxed{}$

$6 \times \boxed{} = 24$

$\boxed{} \times 4 = 44$

$2 \times 4 = \boxed{}$

$1 \times \boxed{} = 4$

$4 \times 4 = \boxed{}$

$\boxed{} \times 4 = 12$

$5 \times \boxed{} = 20$

$\boxed{} \times 4 = 48$

$8 \times 4 = \boxed{}$

$9 \times \boxed{} = 36$

$\boxed{} \times 4 = 28$

Did you know ... ?

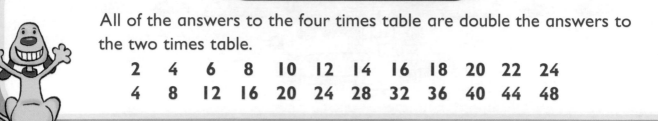

All of the answers to the four times table are double the answers to the two times table.

2	4	6	8	10	12	14	16	18	20	22	24
4	8	12	16	20	24	28	32	36	40	44	48

1 Every number put into the number machine is doubled and then doubled again.

Fill in the missing numbers.

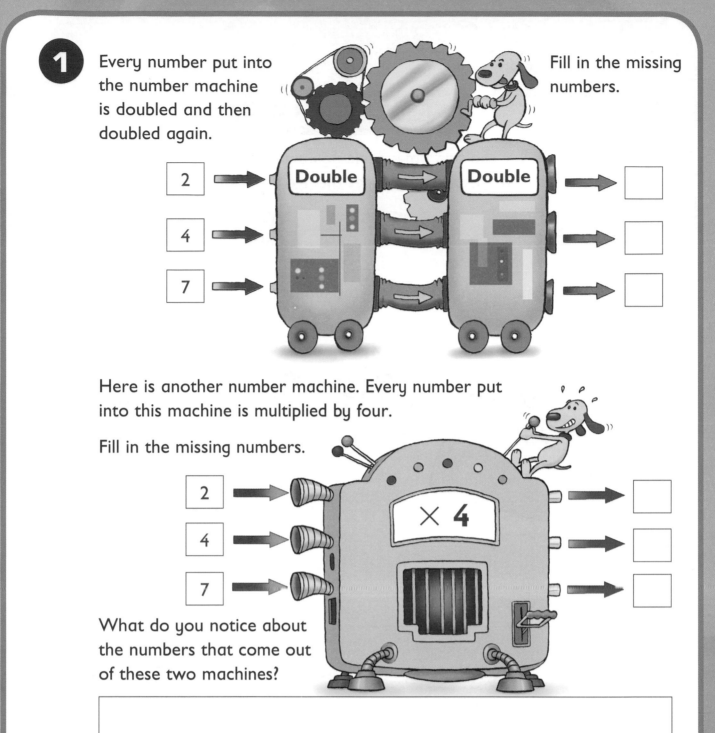

2	→	Double	→	Double	→	☐
4	→				→	☐
7	→				→	☐

Here is another number machine. Every number put into this machine is multiplied by four.

Fill in the missing numbers.

2	→	× 4	→	☐
4	→		→	☐
7	→		→	☐

What do you notice about the numbers that come out of these two machines?

_____

2 Colour a path that only goes through answers to the four times table.

1	13	23	34	6	48	→ Finish
3	32	40	36	8	4	
24	28	15	29	18	11	
12	27	5	7	9	38	
Start → 16	22	17	14	19	25	

Mixed tables

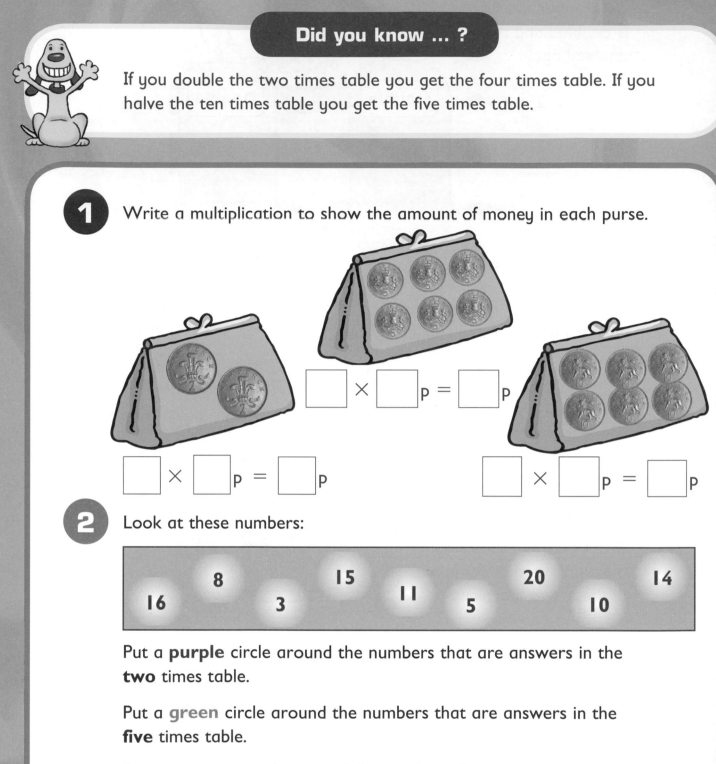

1 Write a multiplication to show the amount of money in each purse.

☐ × ☐ p = ☐ p

☐ × ☐ p = ☐ p

☐ × ☐ p = ☐ p

2 Look at these numbers:

16   8   3   15   11   5   20   10   14

Put a **purple** circle around the numbers that are answers in the **two** times table.

Put a **green** circle around the numbers that are answers in the **five** times table.

Put an **orange** circle around the numbers that are answers in the **ten** times table.

Which numbers have three different coloured rings around them?   ☐ and ☐

Which numbers do not have any rings around them?   ☐ and ☐

3 Every number put into the number machine is first multiplied by 2 and then by 5.

Fill in the missing numbers.

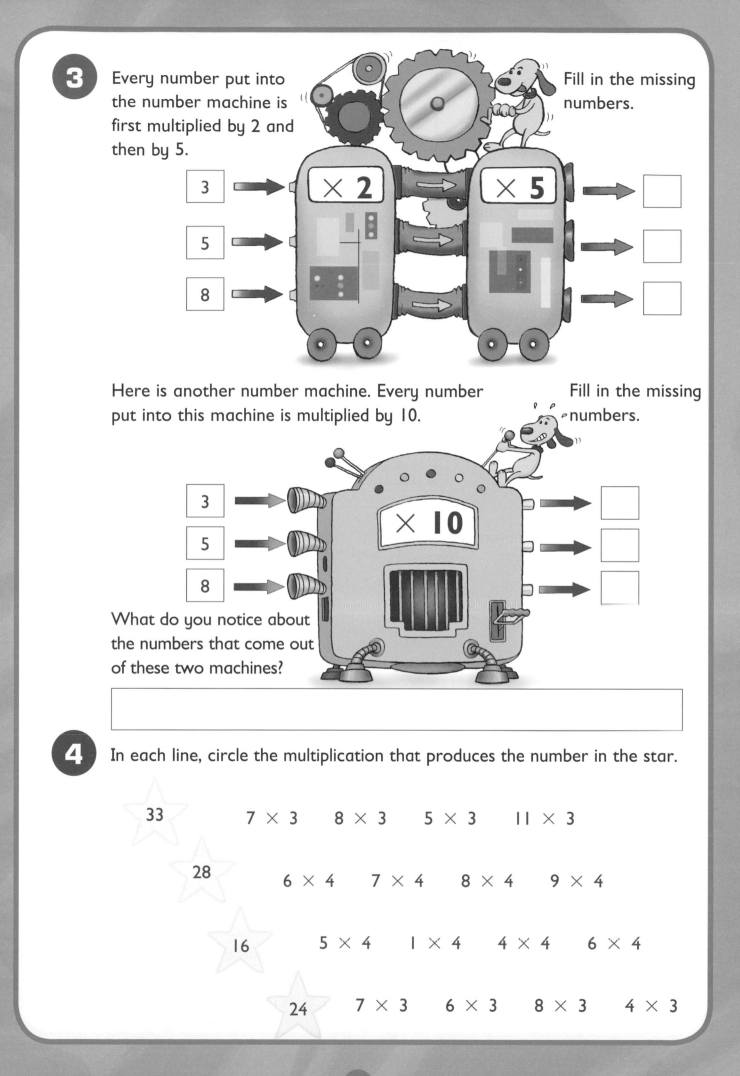

3 → × 2 → → × 5 → ☐

5 → → ☐

8 → → ☐

Here is another number machine. Every number put into this machine is multiplied by 10.

Fill in the missing numbers.

3 → × 10 → ☐

5 → ☐

8 → ☐

What do you notice about the numbers that come out of these two machines?

4 In each line, circle the multiplication that produces the number in the star.

33   7 × 3   8 × 3   5 × 3   11 × 3

28   6 × 4   7 × 4   8 × 4   9 × 4

16   5 × 4   1 × 4   4 × 4   6 × 4

24   7 × 3   6 × 3   8 × 3   4 × 3

5 Colour in **red** every shape that contains an answer to the **four** times table.

Colour in **blue** every shape that contains an answer to the **three** times table.

What do you see?

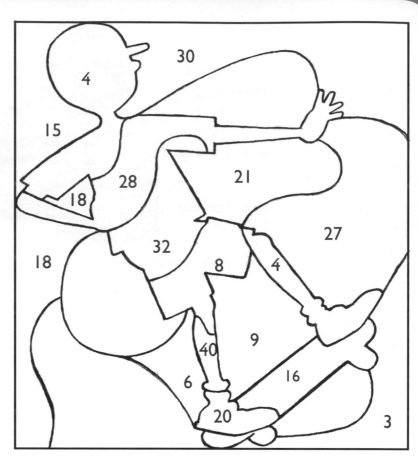

6 An adult rollercoaster ticket costs £5.

A child rollercoaster ticket costs £3.

How much would it cost to buy:

5 adult tickets £ ☐

7 adult tickets £ ☐

12 adult tickets £ ☐

3 child tickets £ ☐

2 child tickets £ ☐

10 child tickets £ ☐

How many child tickets can you buy for £21? ☐

7 Choose the correct answer for each multiplication question.

Colour the letter next to that answer.

6	×	4	=	24	c	or	26	t
8	×	3	=	32	h	or	24	r
9	×	2	=	16	i	or	18	e
7	×	5	=	35	p	or	45	r
4	×	10	=	40	a	or	80	t
8	×	4	=	36	y	or	32	s

The letters you have **not** coloured
spell out the name of a number.

What is the number?

8 Answer these questions.

Multiply five by ten.

Double four.

What is 7 multiplied by 3?

Multiply four by itself.

Divide 24 by 4.

How many threes are there in 27?

What is the twelfth multiple of five?

How many fives are there in forty-five?

Six times table

Read the six times table out loud.

$1 \times 6 = 6$

$2 \times 6 = 12$

$3 \times 6 = 18$

$4 \times 6 = 24$

$5 \times 6 = 30$

$6 \times 6 = 36$

$7 \times 6 = 42$

$8 \times 6 = 48$

$9 \times 6 = 54$

$10 \times 6 = 60$

$11 \times 6 = 66$

$12 \times 6 = 72$

Now fill in these answers.

$5 \times 6 = \boxed{}$

$\boxed{} \times 6 = 36$

$7 \times \boxed{} = 42$

$\boxed{} \times 6 = 66$

$2 \times 6 = \boxed{}$

$\boxed{} \times 6 = 18$

$10 \times \boxed{} = 60$

$\boxed{} \times 6 = 6$

$9 \times \boxed{} = 54$

$4 \times 6 = \boxed{}$

$8 \times \boxed{} = 48$

$12 \times 6 = \boxed{}$

Did you know ... ?

Each answer in the six times table is double that in the three times table.

3	6	9	12	15	18	21	24	27	30	33	36
6	12	18	24	30	36	42	48	54	60	66	72

1 Find a path through the maze that only passes through numbers in the six times table.

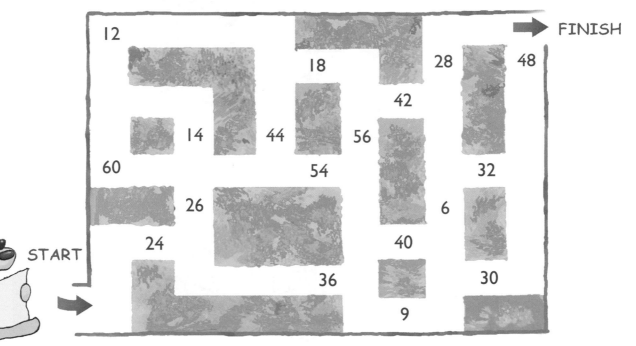

2 Choose the correct answer for each multiplication question. Colour the letter next to that answer.

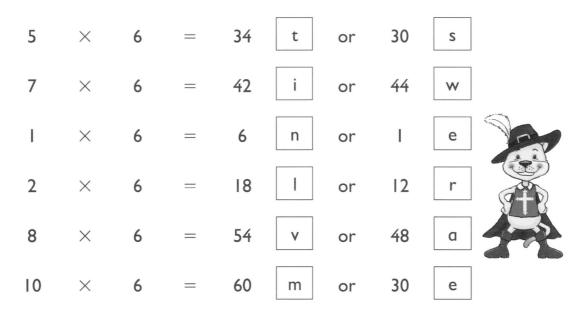

5	×	6	=	34	t	or	30	s
7	×	6	=	42	i	or	44	w
1	×	6	=	6	n	or	1	e
2	×	6	=	18	l	or	12	r
8	×	6	=	54	v	or	48	a
10	×	6	=	60	m	or	30	e

The letters that you have **not** coloured spell out the name of a number.

What is the number?

This number is the product of which multiplication in the six times table?

Did you know ... ?

To find the product of two numbers you multiply them together.

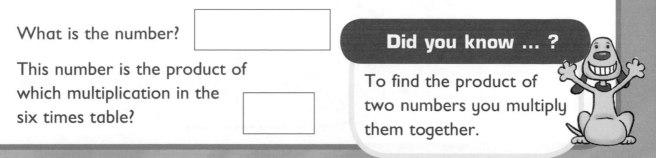

3 Draw a line to match each key to its door.

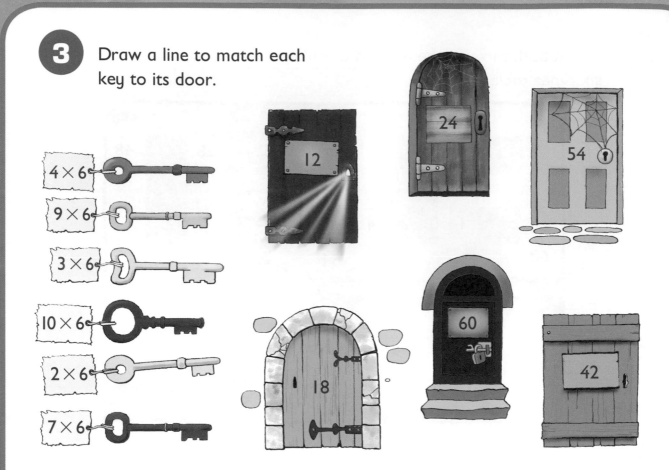

4×6
9×6
3×6
10×6
2×6
7×6

12
24
54
18
60
42

4 Every number put into the number machine is multiplied by six.

Fill in the missing numbers.

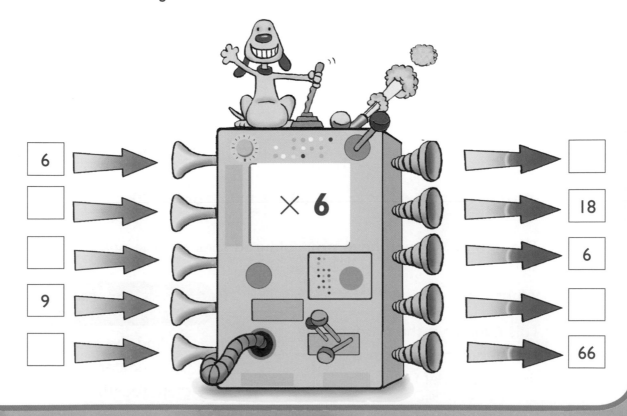

6 →
→
→
9 →
→

$\times 6$

→
→ 18
→ 6
→
→ 66

5 Here are some clothes for sale in a shop.

£3   £4   £8   £12   £1

How much is six caps?   £ ☐

How much is six T-shirts?   £ ☐

How much is six jumpers?   £ ☐

How much is six pairs of socks? £ ☐

How much is six pairs of jeans? £ ☐

6 A treasure chest holds six bars of gold.

Write a multiplication to show the number of gold bars in each group of treasure chests.

☐ × ☐ = ☐

☐ × ☐ = ☐

☐ × ☐ = ☐

☐ × ☐ = ☐

☐ × ☐ = ☐

Seven times table

Read the seven times table out loud.

$1 \times 7 = 7$

$2 \times 7 = 14$

$3 \times 7 = 21$

$4 \times 7 = 28$

$5 \times 7 = 35$

$6 \times 7 = 42$

$7 \times 7 = 49$

$8 \times 7 = 56$

$9 \times 7 = 63$

$10 \times 7 = 70$

$11 \times 7 = 77$

$12 \times 7 = 84$

Now fill in these answers.

$9 \times \boxed{} = 63$

$\boxed{} \times 7 = 77$

$8 \times 7 = \boxed{}$

$4 \times 7 = \boxed{}$

$\boxed{} \times 7 = 35$

$10 \times \boxed{} = 70$

$12 \times 7 = \boxed{}$

$\boxed{} \times 7 = 21$

$6 \times \boxed{} = 42$

$7 \times \boxed{} = 49$

$2 \times 7 = \boxed{}$

$\boxed{} \times 7 = 7$

Did you know ... ?

In the seven times table, each of the first ten answers has a different units digit:

7   14   21   28   35   42   49   56   63   70

The pattern repeats itself for the next ten answers **77 84 . . .**

1 Shade in every shape that has an answer to the seven times table.

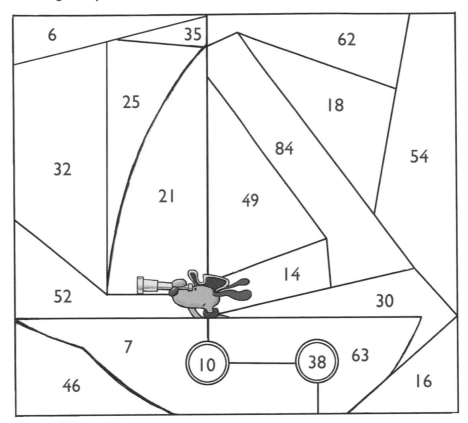

What do you see?

2 There are seven days in one week.

Write multiplications to show the number of days for each number of weeks.

☐ × ☐ = ☐ days

☐ × ☐ = ☐ days

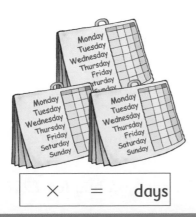

☐ × ☐ = ☐ days

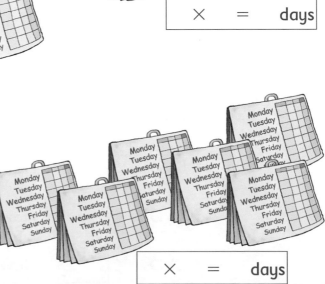

☐ × ☐ = ☐ days

3 Find a path across the river using the stepping stones.

You can only step on stones that are answers in the seven times table.

Colour the path you used.

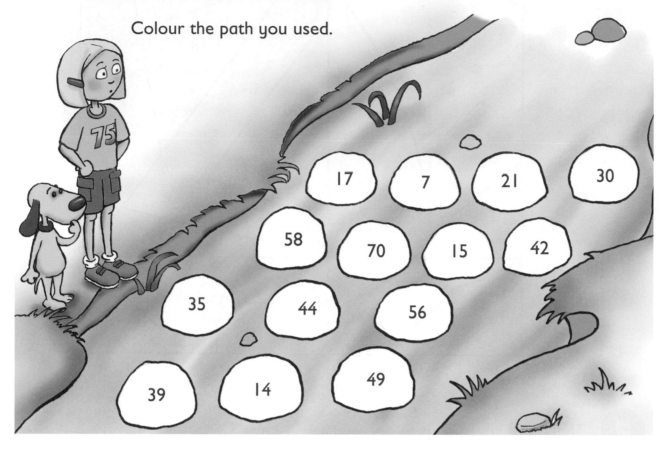

4 A DVD costs £7.

How much will it cost to buy:

5 DVDs   £ ____

8 DVDs   £ ____   How many DVDs can you buy for £35? ____

11 DVDs £ ____   How many DVDs can you buy for £14? ____

9 DVDs   £ ____   How many DVDs can you buy for £49? ____

4 DVDs   £ ____   How many DVDs can you buy for £21? ____

5 Every number put into the number machine is multiplied by seven.

Fill in the missing numbers.

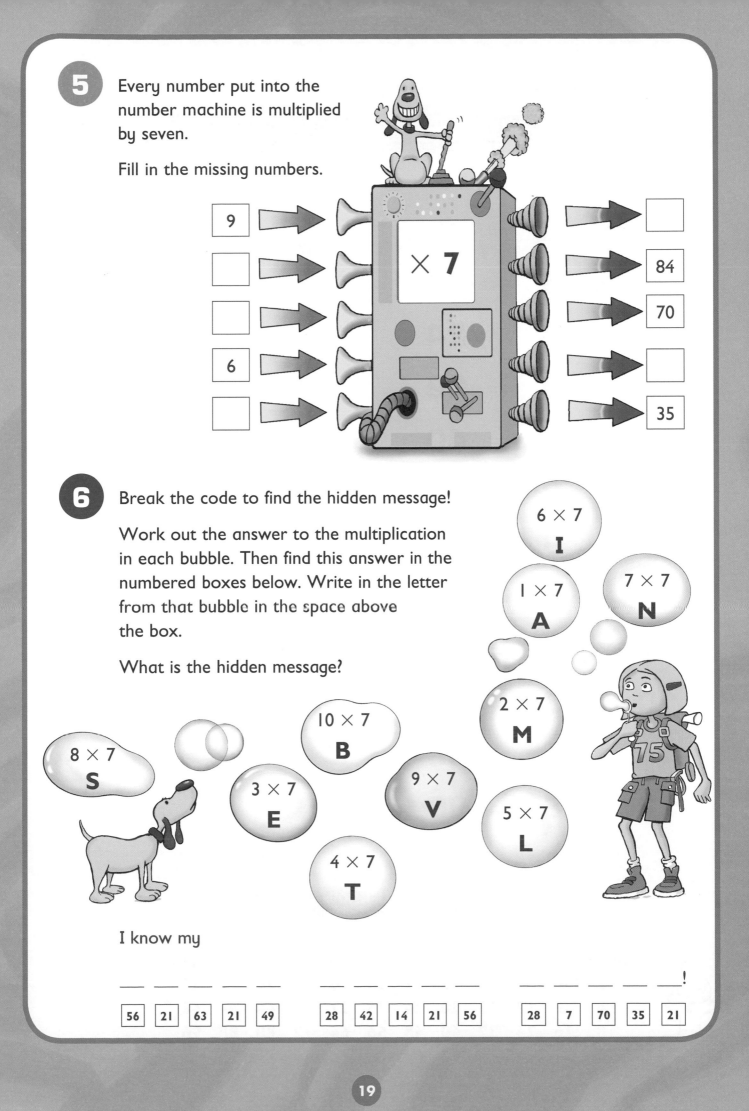

9 →

□ → 84

□ → 70

6 →

□ → 35

□ →
□ →
□ →

× 7

6 Break the code to find the hidden message!

Work out the answer to the multiplication in each bubble. Then find this answer in the numbered boxes below. Write in the letter from that bubble in the space above the box.

What is the hidden message?

6 × 7
I

1 × 7
A

7 × 7
N

2 × 7
M

8 × 7
S

10 × 7
B

3 × 7
E

9 × 7
V

5 × 7
L

4 × 7
T

I know my

___ ___ ___ ___ ___   ___ ___ ___ ___ ___   ___ ___ ___ ___ ___ !

| 56 | 21 | 63 | 21 | 49 | | 28 | 42 | 14 | 21 | 56 | | 28 | 7 | 70 | 35 | 21 |

Eight times table

Read the eight times table out loud.

1	×	8	=	8
2	×	8	=	16
3	×	8	=	24
4	×	8	=	32
5	×	8	=	40
6	×	8	=	48
7	×	8	=	56
8	×	8	=	64
9	×	8	=	72
10	×	8	=	80
11	×	8	=	88
12	×	8	=	96

Now fill in these answers.

7 × ☐ = 56

2 × 8 = ☐

☐ × 8 = 32

9 × ☐ = 72

5 × 8 = ☐

☐ × 8 = 8

8 × ☐ = 64

☐ × 8 = 88

10 × 8 = ☐

☐ × 8 = 24

12 × ☐ = 96

6 × 8 = ☐

Did you know ... ?

You can work out the answers to the eight times table by doubling the four times table (which is already double the two times table):

2	4	6	8	10	12	14	16	18	20	22	24
4	8	12	16	20	24	28	32	36	40	44	48
8	16	24	32	40	48	56	64	72	80	88	96

1 Work out the answers to each multiplication. Then use the answers to find the correct colour in the code key.

Colour the picture.

Code key	
8, 48, 64	= blue
72	= grey
32	= red
56	= yellow
24	= green
40	= purple

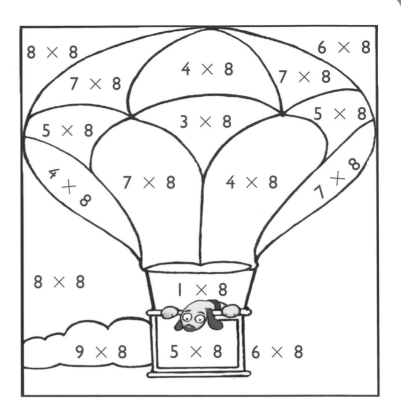

2 Colour all the squares that have an answer to the eight times table.

1	2	3	4	5	6	7	8	9	10
11	12	13	14	15	16	17	18	19	20
21	22	23	24	25	26	27	28	29	30
31	32	33	34	35	36	37	38	39	40
41	42	43	44	45	46	47	48	49	50
51	52	53	54	55	56	57	58	59	60
61	62	63	64	65	66	67	68	69	70
71	72	73	74	75	76	77	78	79	80
81	82	83	84	85	86	87	88	89	90
91	92	93	94	95	96	97	98	99	100

3 A spider has eight legs.

Write a multiplication to show the number of legs in each group of spiders.

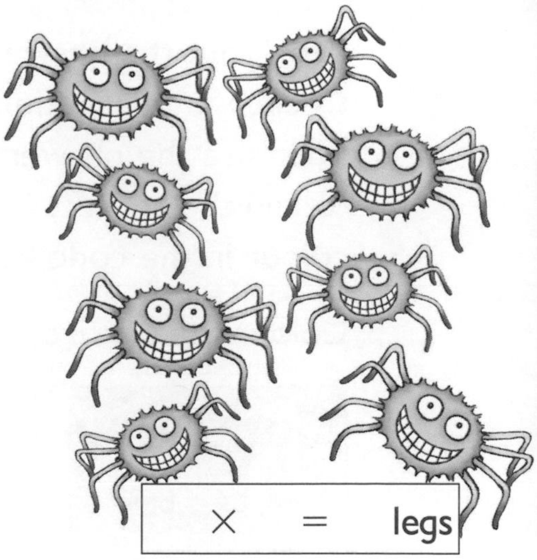

[___ × ___ = ___ legs]

[___ × ___ = ___ legs]

[___ × ___ = ___ legs]

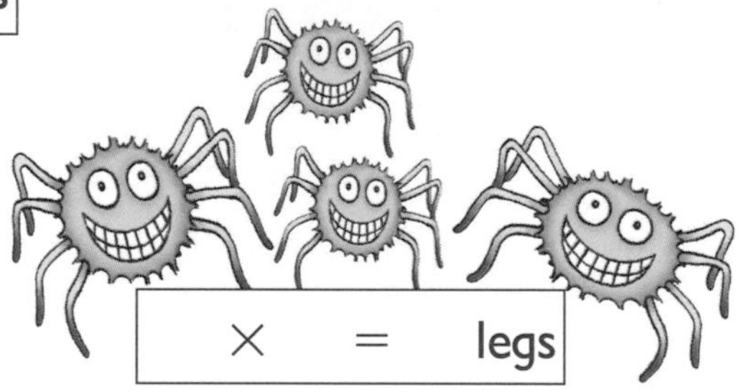

[___ × ___ = ___ legs]

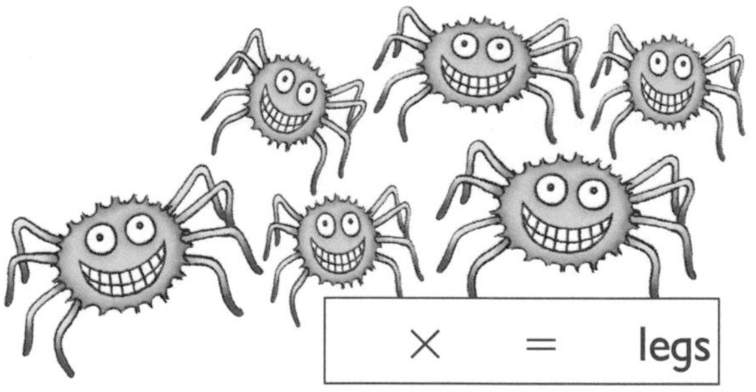

[___ × ___ = ___ legs]

4 Draw a line to match each multiplication to its correct answer.

4 × 8

9 × 8

2 × 8

7 × 8

12 × 8

5 × 8

72

40

56

32

16

96

5 Choose the correct answer for each multiplication question.
Colour the letter next to that answer.

3 × 8 = 22 [e] or 24 [s]

6 × 8 = 56 [i] or 48 [p]

7 × 8 = 56 [x] or 42 [g]

4 × 8 = 32 [a] or 30 [h]

9 × 8 = 74 [t] or 72 [n]

8 × 8 = 60 [y] or 64 [r]

The letters that you have **not** coloured spell out the name of a number.

What is the number? [ ]   This number is the product of

which multiplication in the eight times table? [ ]

6 Answer these questions.

What are four eights? [ ]

What is ten multiplied by eight? [ ]

What is 7 times 8? [ ]

Multiply 11 by 8. [ ]

Which number multiplied by 8 is 8? [ ]

How many eights in forty? [ ]

Divide 48 by 8. [ ]

How many eights in 24? [ ]

Double eight. [ ]

Multiply eight by itself. [ ]

Nine times table

Read the nine times table out loud.

$1 \times 9 = 9$

$2 \times 9 = 18$

$3 \times 9 = 27$

$4 \times 9 = 36$

$5 \times 9 = 45$

$6 \times 9 = 54$

$7 \times 9 = 63$

$8 \times 9 = 72$

$9 \times 9 = 81$

$10 \times 9 = 90$

$11 \times 9 = 99$

$12 \times 9 = 108$

Now fill in these answers.

$\boxed{} \times 9 = 9$

$11 \times \boxed{} = 99$

$8 \times 9 = \boxed{}$

$3 \times \boxed{} = 27$

$\boxed{} \times 9 = 90$

$2 \times 9 = \boxed{}$

$5 \times \boxed{} = 45$

$\boxed{} \times 9 = 63$

$4 \times 9 = \boxed{}$

$6 \times \boxed{} = 54$

$\boxed{} \times 9 = 81$

$12 \times 9 = \boxed{}$

Did you know ... ?

The digits in the first ten answers to the nine times table add up to 9:

09 $0 + 9 = 9$ **18** $1 + 8 = 9$ **27** $2 + 7 = 9$ ...

1 A useful way to remember the nine times table is to use your fingers as shown opposite.

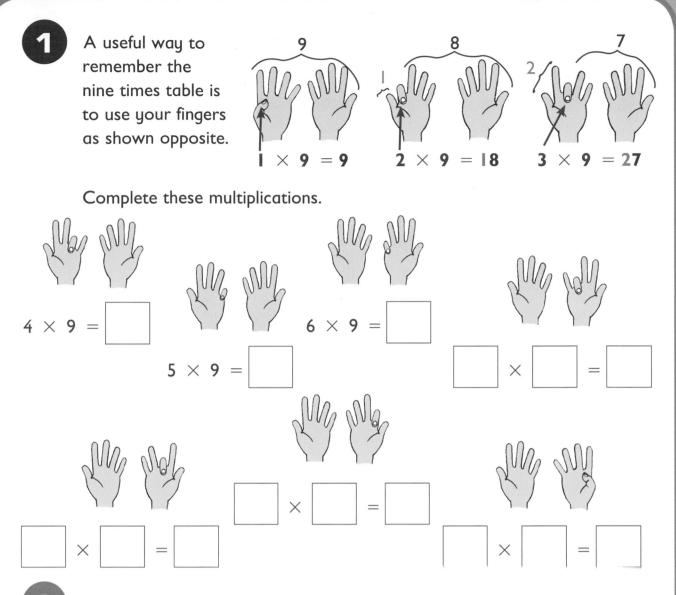

$1 \times 9 = 9$ $2 \times 9 = 18$ $3 \times 9 = 27$

Complete these multiplications.

$4 \times 9 = \boxed{}$

$5 \times 9 = \boxed{}$

$6 \times 9 = \boxed{}$

$\boxed{} \times \boxed{} = \boxed{}$

$\boxed{} \times \boxed{} = \boxed{}$

$\boxed{} \times \boxed{} = \boxed{}$

$\boxed{} \times \boxed{} = \boxed{}$

2 Work out the answers to each multiplication. Then use the answers to find the correct colour in the code key.

Colour the picture.

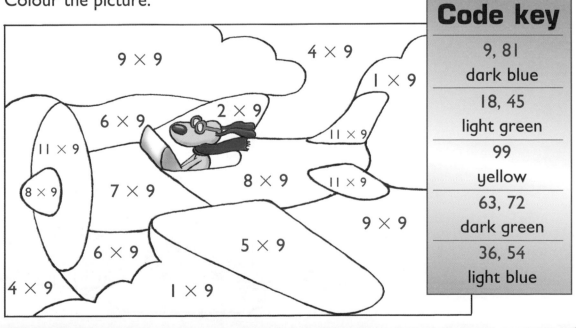

Code key
9, 81 dark blue
18, 45 light green
99 yellow
63, 72 dark green
36, 54 light blue

Picture labels: 9×9, 4×9, 1×9, 6×9, 2×9, 11×9, 11×9, 11×9, 8×9, 7×9, 8×9, 9×9, 6×9, 5×9, 4×9, 1×9

3 Break the code to find the hidden word!

Work out the answer to the multiplication in each bubble. Then find this answer in the numbered boxes below. Write in the letter from that bubble in the space above the box.

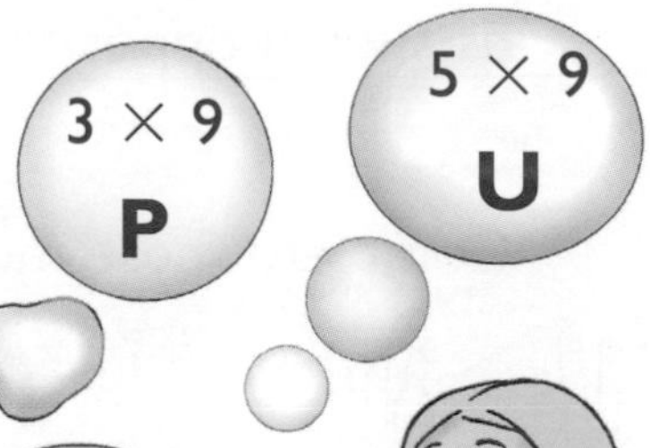

What is the hidden word?

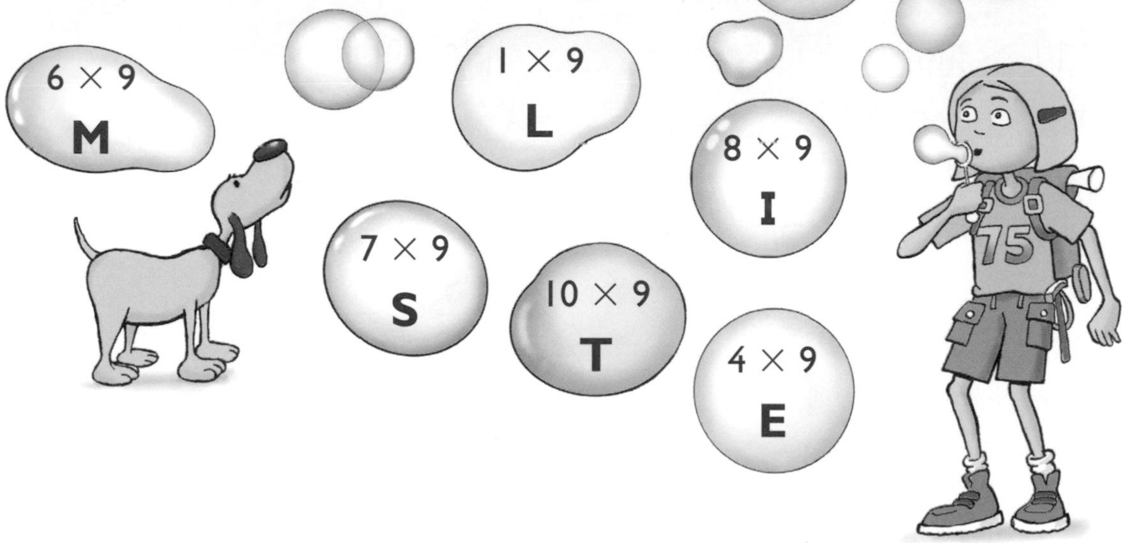

3 × 9 **P**

5 × 9 **U**

6 × 9 **M**

1 × 9 **L**

8 × 9 **I**

7 × 9 **S**

10 × 9 **T**

4 × 9 **E**

| 54 | 45 | 9 | 90 | 72 | 27 | 9 | 36 | 63 |

4 Every number put into the number machine is multiplied by nine.

Fill in the missing numbers.

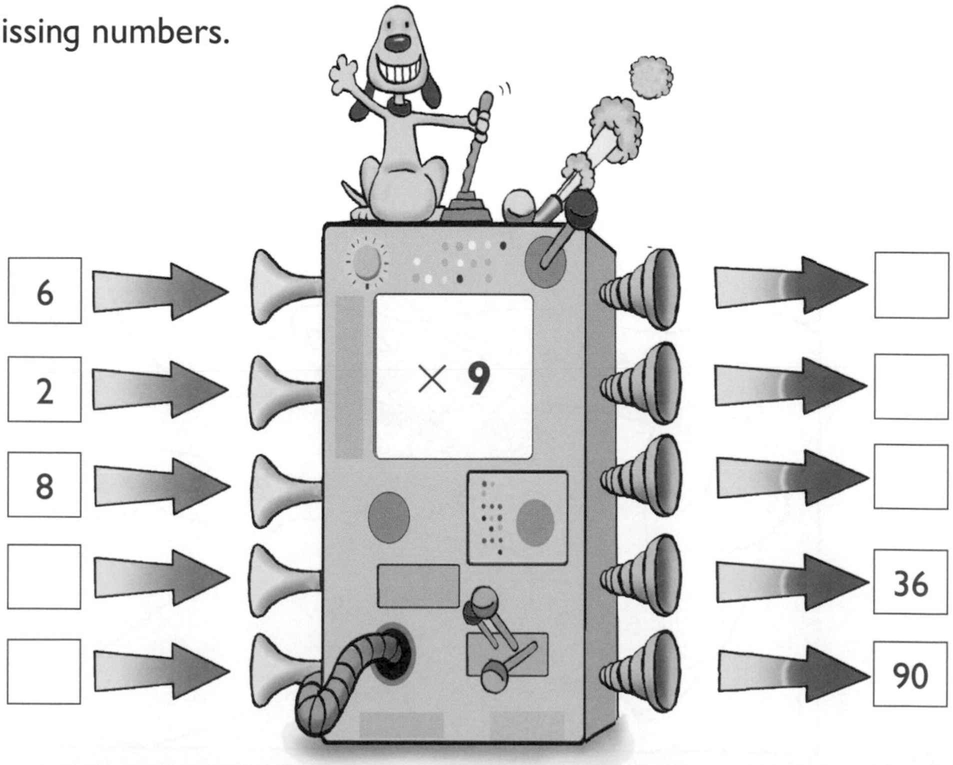

× 9

6 →

2 →

8 →

☐ →

☐ →

→ ☐

→ ☐

→ ☐

→ 36

→ 90

5 Find a path through the maze. You can only go through numbers which are answers in the nine times table.

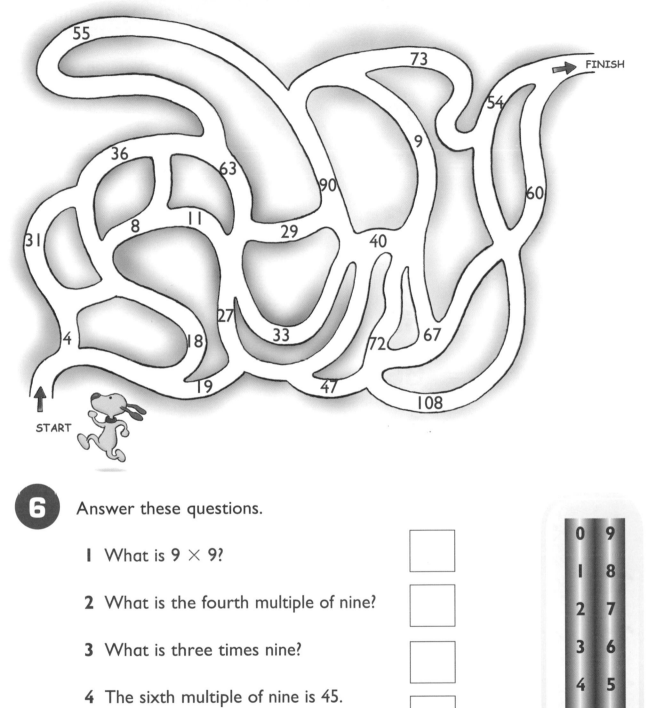

55
73
FINISH
54
9
36
63
90
60
11
8
29
40
31
27
33
72
67
4
18
19
47
108
START

6 Answer these questions.

1 What is 9×9?

2 What is the fourth multiple of nine?

3 What is three times nine?

4 The sixth multiple of nine is 45. Is this true or false?

0	9
1	8
2	7
3	6
4	5
5	4
6	3
7	2
8	1
9	0

Did you know ... ?

If you write down the first ten **multiples of nine** in two columns you will see a pattern that makes it easy to remember them.

Eleven times table

Read the eleven times table out loud.

1 × **11** = **11**

2 × **11** = **22**

3 × **11** = **33**

4 × **11** = **44**

5 × **11** = **55**

6 × **11** = **66**

7 × **11** = **77**

8 × **11** = **88**

9 × **11** = **99**

10 × **11** = **110**

11 × **11** = **121**

12 × **11** = **132**

Now fill in these answers.

4 × ☐ = 44

☐ × 11 = 110

1 × 11 = ☐

6 × ☐ = 66

☐ × 11 = 88

12 × 11 = ☐

2 × ☐ = 22

☐ × 11 = 55

9 × 11 = ☐

☐ × 11 = 77

11 × ☐ = 121

3 × 11 = ☐

Did you know ... ?

The first nine answers in the eleven times table are easy to remember. Simply repeat the digit:

11   22   33   44   55   66   77   88   99

1 Every number put into the number machine is multiplied by eleven.

Fill in the missing numbers.

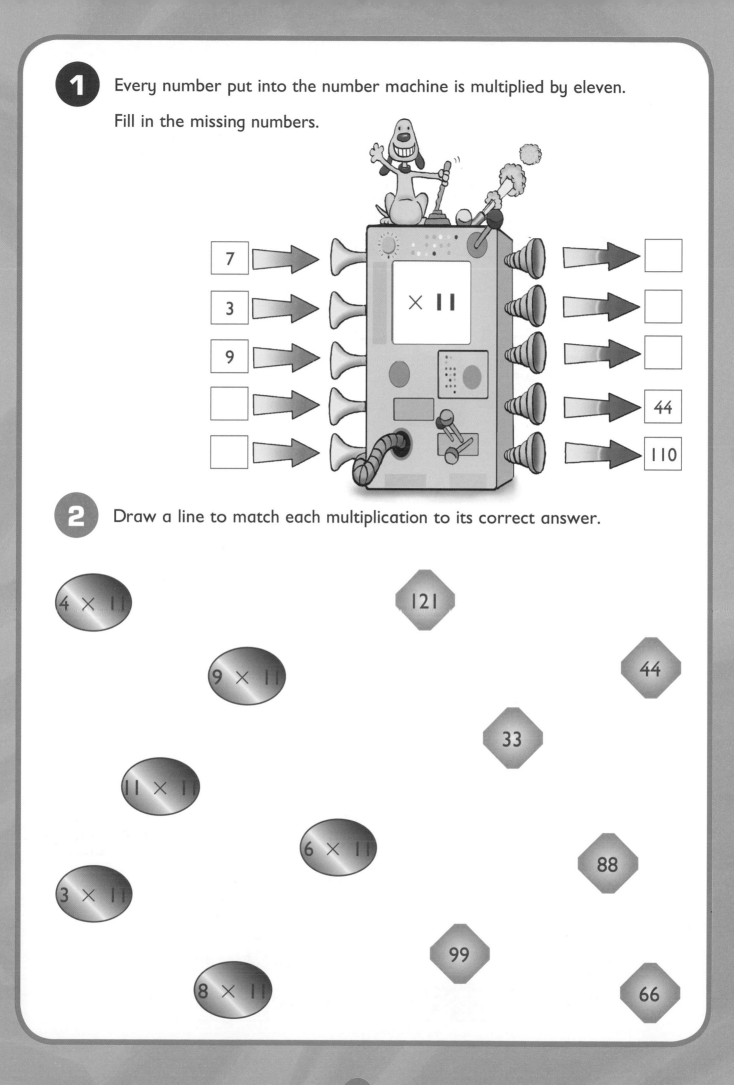

7 →
3 →
9 →
☐ →
☐ →

→ ☐
→ ☐
→ ☐
→ 44
→ 110

2 Draw a line to match each multiplication to its correct answer.

4 × 11

9 × 11

11 × 11

6 × 11

3 × 11

8 × 11

121

44

33

88

99

66

29

3 There are 11 players in one football team.

Write multiplications to show the number of players for each group of teams.

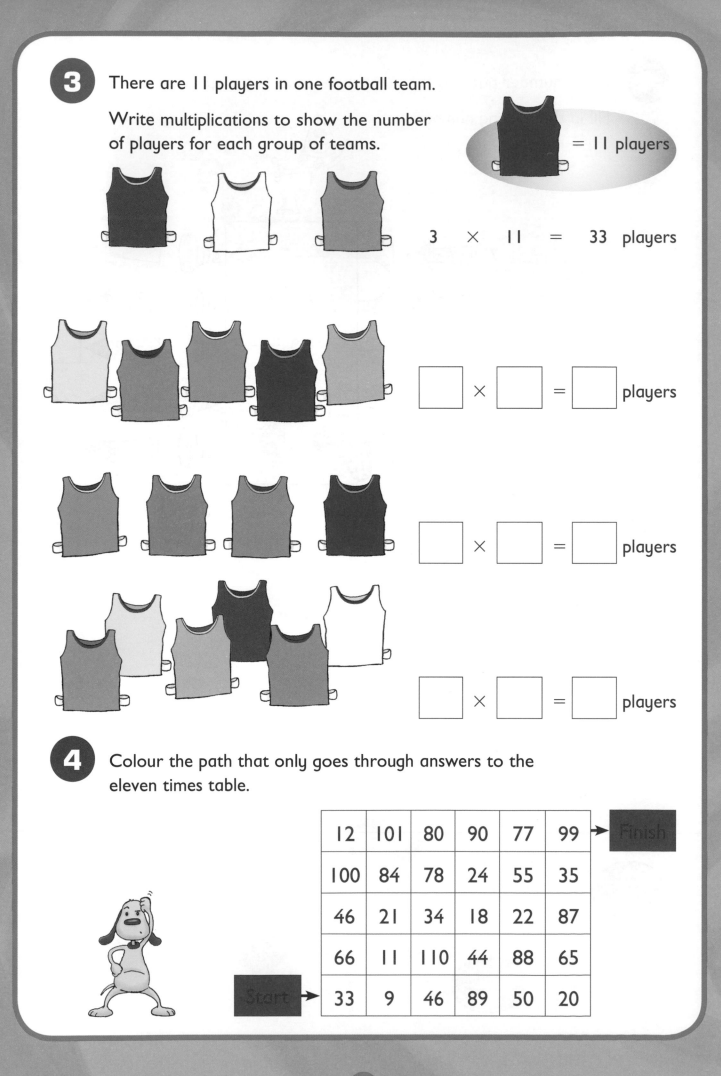

= 11 players

3 × 11 = 33 players

☐ × ☐ = ☐ players

☐ × ☐ = ☐ players

☐ × ☐ = ☐ players

4 Colour the path that only goes through answers to the eleven times table.

12	101	80	90	77	99	Finish
100	84	78	24	55	35	
46	21	34	18	22	87	
66	11	110	44	88	65	
Start → 33	9	46	89	50	20	

5 Answer these questions.

What is 12 × 11? ☐

How many elevens are in 66? ☐

Double 11. ☐

What is the product of 3 and 11? ☐

An apple costs 11p. I have 55p.
How many apples can I buy? ☐

The third multiple of the
eleven times table is 44.
True or false? ☐

Multiply eleven by seven. ☐

What is 11 multiplied by itself? ☐

6 In each line circle the multiplication that produces the number in the box.

| 55 | 6 × 11 | 4 × 11 | 5 × 11 | 10 × 11 |

| 88 | 8 × 11 | 4 × 11 | 9 × 11 | 7 × 11 |

| 44 | 5 × 11 | 2 × 11 | 6 × 11 | 4 × 11 |

| 110 | 1 × 11 | 10 × 11 | 11 × 11 | 8 × 11 |

Twelve times table

Read the twelve times table out loud.

1 × 12 = 12

2 × 12 = 24

3 × 12 = 36

4 × 12 = 48

5 × 12 = 60

6 × 12 = 72

7 × 12 = 84

8 × 12 = 96

9 × 12 = 108

10 × 12 = 120

11 × 12 = 132

12 × 12 = 144

Now fill in these answers.

9 × 12 = ☐

3 × ☐ = 36

☐ × 12 = 144

1 × ☐ = 12

☐ × 12 = 96

5 × 12 = ☐

2 × ☐ = 24

☐ × 12 = 132

6 × 12 = ☐

10 × ☐ = 120

☐ × 12 = 84

4 × 12 = ☐

Did you know ... ?

All answers in the twelve times table are even numbers. The last digits have the pattern: **2, 4, 6, 8, 0 ...**

12   24   36   48   60   72   84   96   108   120   132   144

1 Colour in every shape that contains an answer to the twelve times table.

What do you see?

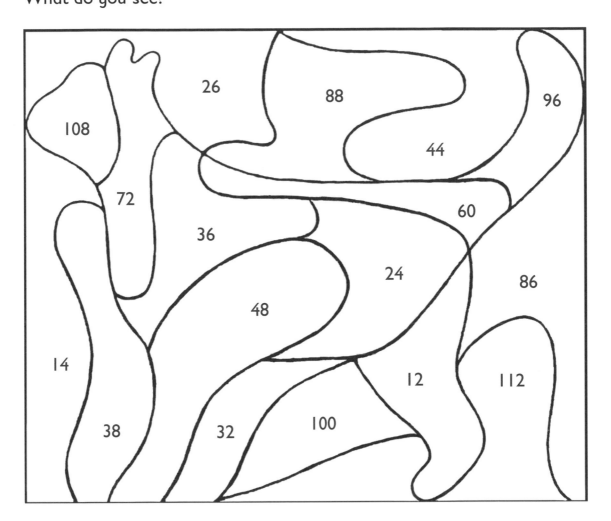

2 Here are some multiplications. Some are correct and some are wrong.

Tick those that show the correct answer. Put a cross next to those that show the wrong answer.

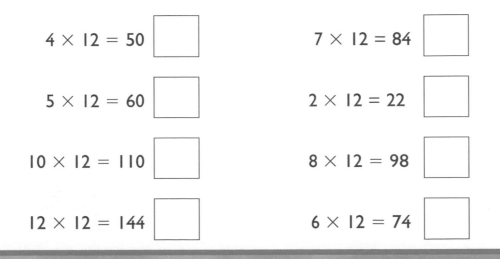

4 × 12 = 50 ☐   7 × 12 = 84 ☐

5 × 12 = 60 ☐   2 × 12 = 22 ☐

10 × 12 = 110 ☐   8 × 12 = 98 ☐

12 × 12 = 144 ☐   6 × 12 = 74 ☐

3 A box holds twelve eggs.

Write a multiplication to show the number of eggs in the egg boxes.

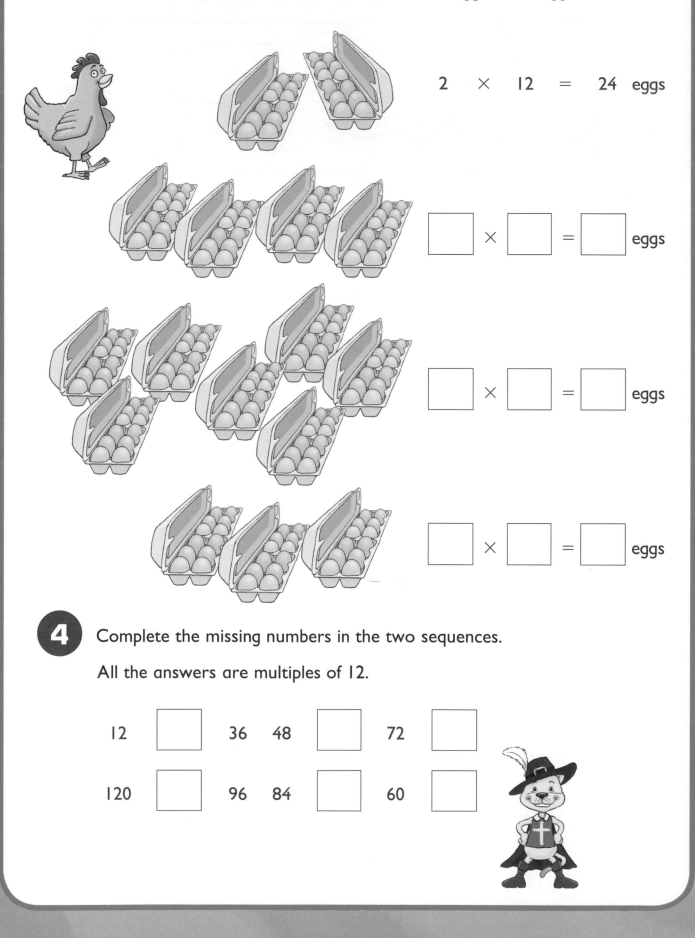

2 $\times$ 12 = 24 eggs

☐ $\times$ ☐ = ☐ eggs

☐ $\times$ ☐ = ☐ eggs

☐ $\times$ ☐ = ☐ eggs

4 Complete the missing numbers in the two sequences.

All the answers are multiples of 12.

12   ☐   36   48   ☐   72   ☐

120   ☐   96   84   ☐   60   ☐

5 Work out the answer to each multiplication to complete the table.

Use the code to replace each number below with the correct letter and make words.

3	×	12		a
6	×	12		e
2	×	12		i
1	×	12		u
7	×	12		m
8	×	12		l
4	×	12		p
11	×	12		r

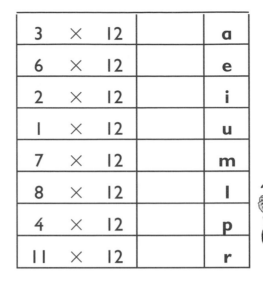

____ ____ ____ ____

96	24	84	72

____ ____ ____ ____

48	96	12	84

____ ____ ____ ____

48	72	36	132

____ ____ ____ ____ ____

36	48	48	96	72

What do these words have in common?

_____

_____

_____

6 A belt costs £12.

How much would it cost to buy:

4 belts £ [ ]

10 belts £ [ ]

7 belts £ [ ]

12 belts £ [ ]

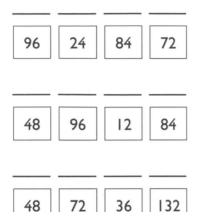

Mixed tables

1 Here are some number machines. Fill in the missing number on the machine.

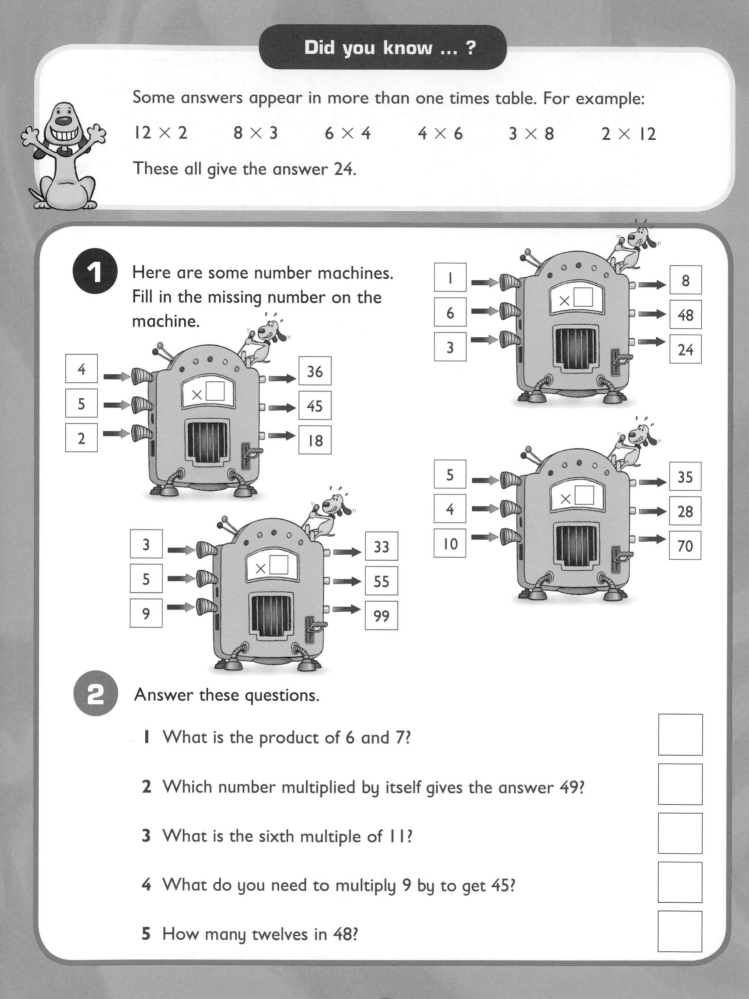

2 Answer these questions.

1 What is the product of 6 and 7?

2 Which number multiplied by itself gives the answer 49?

3 What is the sixth multiple of 11?

4 What do you need to multiply 9 by to get 45?

5 How many twelves in 48?

3 This is a zig-zag multiplication snake.

Work out each multiplication and write the answer in the grid.

The last digit of each answer is the first digit of the next answer.

The first two have been filled in for you.

1	9 × 4	9	9 × 5
2	8 × 8	10	7 × 8
3	6 × 8	11	9 × 7
4	9 × 9	12	8 × 4
5	7 × 2	13	9 × 3
6	7 × 6	14	8 × 9
7	5 × 5	15	5 × 4
8	6 × 9		

4 Count on or back for each row of times tables.

60	54							6
7		21		35		49		63	70
88	80			56			24	
9			36			63			90
144	132				84		60		36

5 Look at the numbers below.

7   32   21   70

                              24

42   49

                    30   40

      48

6   56   63   16

Circle in **red** the multiples of 7.
Circle in **orange** the multiples of 8.

Which number have you circled twice? ☐

6 A multi-monster has **three** heads, **six** eyes, **nine** ears and **four** arms.

How many heads, eyes, ears and arms are there on:

3 multi-monsters?

☐ heads   ☐ eyes

☐ ears   ☐ arms

10 multi-monsters?

☐ heads   ☐ eyes

☐ ears   ☐ arms

7 multi-monsters?

☐ heads   ☐ eyes

☐ ears   ☐ arms

7 Here are some targets.

If an arrow lands in the outer-most blue ring it scores 2 times (double) the number.

If it lands in the middle yellow ring it scores 3 times (treble) the number.

If it lands in the inner-most red ring it scores 10 times the number.

Write down the score for each target.

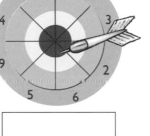

$7 \times 2 = 14$

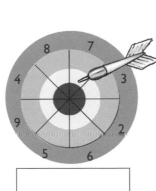

8 Match each product to its correct answer.

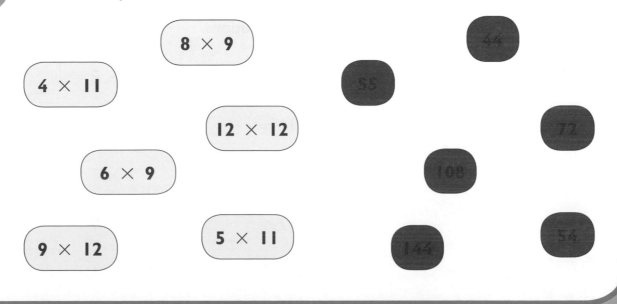

8×9

4×11

12×12

6×9

9×12

5×11

44

55

72

108

144

54

9 Here are some items for sale in the toy shop.

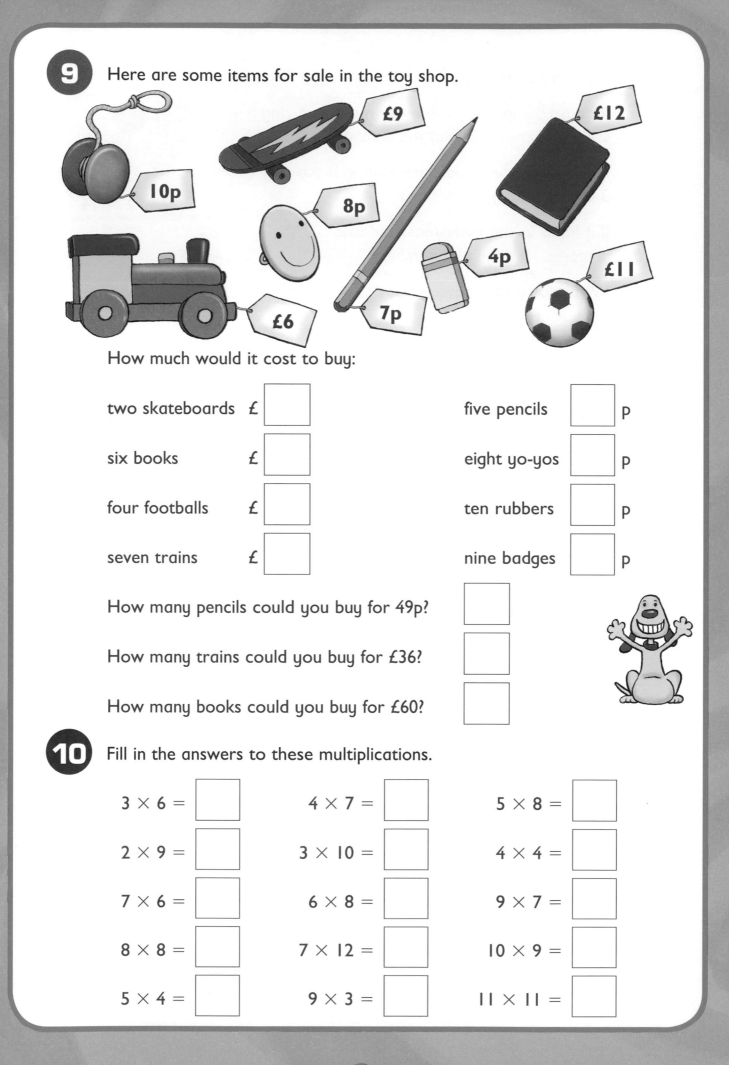

How much would it cost to buy:

two skateboards £ ☐

six books £ ☐

four footballs £ ☐

seven trains £ ☐

five pencils ☐ p

eight yo-yos ☐ p

ten rubbers ☐ p

nine badges ☐ p

How many pencils could you buy for 49p? ☐

How many trains could you buy for £36? ☐

How many books could you buy for £60? ☐

10 Fill in the answers to these multiplications.

3 × 6 = ☐   4 × 7 = ☐   5 × 8 = ☐

2 × 9 = ☐   3 × 10 = ☐   4 × 4 = ☐

7 × 6 = ☐   6 × 8 = ☐   9 × 7 = ☐

8 × 8 = ☐   7 × 12 = ☐   10 × 9 = ☐

5 × 4 = ☐   9 × 3 = ☐   11 × 11 = ☐

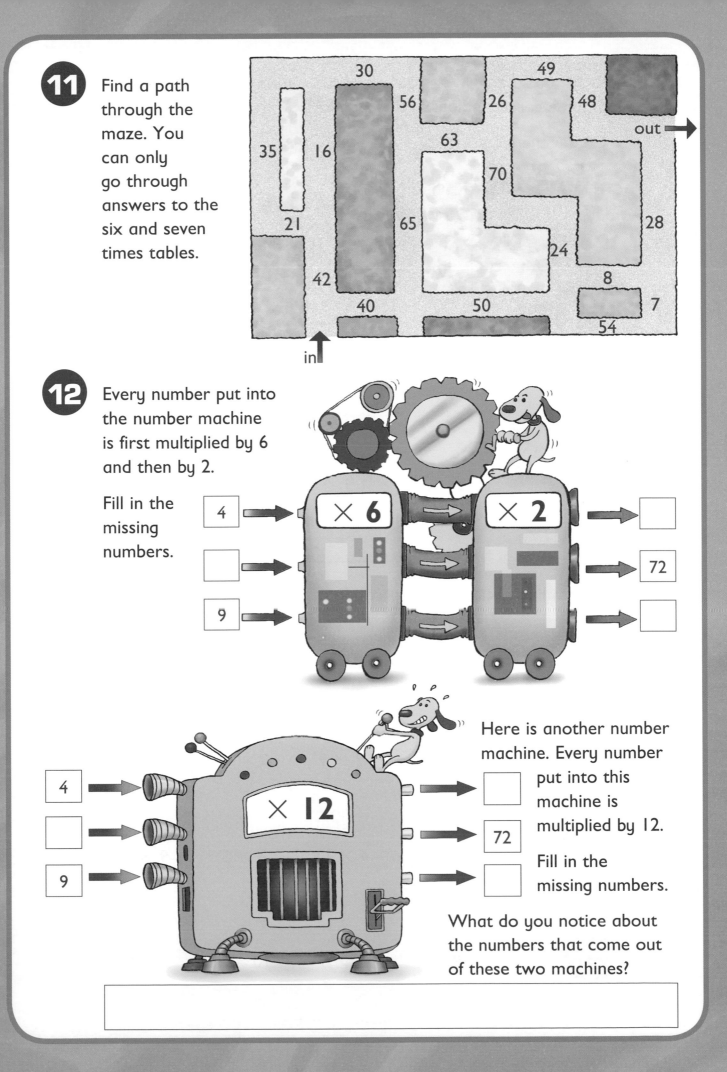

11 Find a path through the maze. You can only go through answers to the six and seven times tables.

30   49
56   26   48
        out →
35   16
        63
        70
21
65   28
            24
42   8
40   50   7
        54
in

12 Every number put into the number machine is first multiplied by 6 and then by 2.

Fill in the missing numbers.

4 → × 6 → × 2 →

→ → 72

9 → →

4 →

→

9 → × 12

→

72

→

Here is another number machine. Every number put into this machine is multiplied by 12.

Fill in the missing numbers.

What do you notice about the numbers that come out of these two machines?

13 Work out the answers to each multiplication. Then use the answers to find the correct colour in the code key.

Colour the picture.

Code key	
24	= red
48	= yellow
20	= orange
35	= pink
36	= brown
55	= white

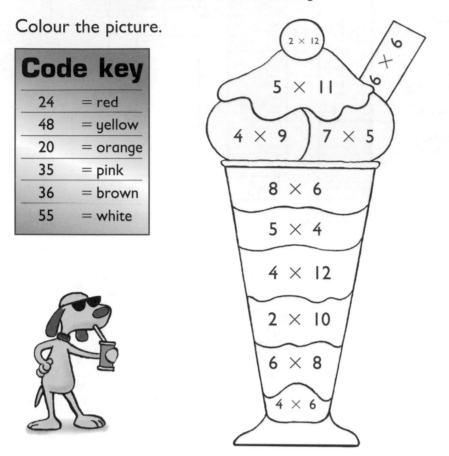

14 In each line circle the multiplication that produces the number in the box.

| **72** | 8 × 9 | 9 × 7 | 8 × 8 | 7 × 12 |

| **63** | 6 × 10 | 7 × 9 | 6 × 11 | 8 × 8 |

| **45** | 9 × 6 | 4 × 11 | 8 × 5 | 9 × 5 |

| **81** | 9 × 7 | 9 × 9 | 10 × 8 | 6 × 12 |

15

Here's a real challenge! Complete the multiplication grid.

x	1	2	3	4	5	6	7	8	9	10	11	12
1	1	2										
2		4										
3			12								33	
4								32				48
5		15										
6						36						
7										70		
8							56					
9									81			
10					50							
11			33									
12						72						

For help on using a multiplication grid, you can look on page 45.

16

Break the code to find the hidden message!

Work out the answer to the multiplication in each bubble. Then find this answer in the numbered boxes below. Write in the letter from that bubble in the space above the box.

What is the hidden message?

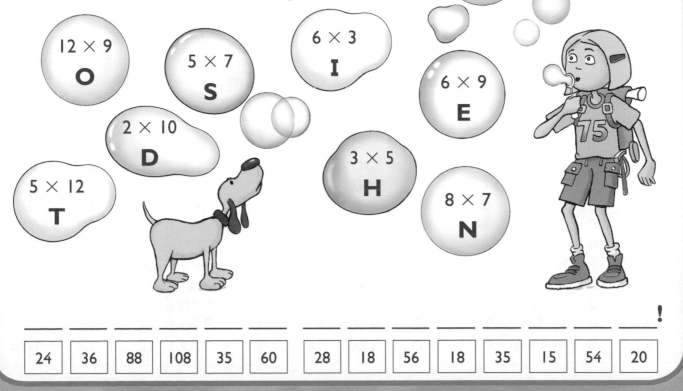

4 × 6 **A**

11 × 8 **M**

9 × 4 **L**

7 × 4 **F**

12 × 9 **O**

5 × 7 **S**

6 × 3 **I**

6 × 9 **E**

2 × 10 **D**

3 × 5 **H**

5 × 12 **T**

8 × 7 **N**

__ __ __ __ __ __ __ __ __ __ __ __ __ __!

24	36	88	108	35	60	28	18	56	18	35	15	54	20

Here are all of the times tables that you need to know.

One times table

1 × 1 = 1
2 × 1 = 2
3 × 1 = 3
4 × 1 = 4
5 × 1 = 5
6 × 1 = 6
7 × 1 = 7
8 × 1 = 8
9 × 1 = 9
10 × 1 = 10
11 × 1 = 11
12 × 1 = 12

Two times table

1 × 2 = 2
2 × 2 = 4
3 × 2 = 6
4 × 2 = 8
5 × 2 = 10
6 × 2 = 12
7 × 2 = 14
8 × 2 = 16
9 × 2 = 18
10 × 2 = 20
11 × 2 = 22
12 × 2 = 24

Three times table

1 × 3 = 3
2 × 3 = 6
3 × 3 = 9
4 × 3 = 12
5 × 3 = 15
6 × 3 = 18
7 × 3 = 21
8 × 3 = 24
9 × 3 = 27
10 × 3 = 30
11 × 3 = 33
12 × 3 = 36

Four times table

1 × 4 = 4
2 × 4 = 8
3 × 4 = 12
4 × 4 = 16
5 × 4 = 20
6 × 4 = 24
7 × 4 = 28
8 × 4 = 32
9 × 4 = 36
10 × 4 = 40
11 × 4 = 44
12 × 4 = 48

Five times table

1 × 5 = 5
2 × 5 = 10
3 × 5 = 15
4 × 5 = 20
5 × 5 = 25
6 × 5 = 30
7 × 5 = 35
8 × 5 = 40
9 × 5 = 45
10 × 5 = 50
11 × 5 = 55
12 × 5 = 60

Six times table

1 × 6 = 6
2 × 6 = 12
3 × 6 = 18
4 × 6 = 24
5 × 6 = 30
6 × 6 = 36
7 × 6 = 42
8 × 6 = 48
9 × 6 = 54
10 × 6 = 60
11 × 6 = 66
12 × 6 = 72

Seven times table

1 × 7 = 7
2 × 7 = 14
3 × 7 = 21
4 × 7 = 28
5 × 7 = 35
6 × 7 = 42
7 × 7 = 49
8 × 7 = 56
9 × 7 = 63
10 × 7 = 70
11 × 7 = 77
12 × 7 = 84

Eight times table

1 × 8 = 8
2 × 8 = 16
3 × 8 = 24
4 × 8 = 32
5 × 8 = 40
6 × 8 = 48
7 × 8 = 56
8 × 8 = 64
9 × 8 = 72
10 × 8 = 80
11 × 8 = 88
12 × 8 = 96

Nine times table

1 × 9 = 9
2 × 9 = 18
3 × 9 = 27
4 × 9 = 36
5 × 9 = 45
6 × 9 = 54
7 × 9 = 63
8 × 9 = 72
9 × 9 = 81
10 × 9 = 90
11 × 9 = 99
12 × 9 = 108

Ten times table

1 × 10 = 10
2 × 10 = 20
3 × 10 = 30
4 × 10 = 40
5 × 10 = 50
6 × 10 = 60
7 × 10 = 70
8 × 10 = 80
9 × 10 = 90
10 × 10 = 100
11 × 10 = 110
12 × 10 = 120

Eleven times table

1 × 11 = 11
2 × 11 = 22
3 × 11 = 33
4 × 11 = 44
5 × 11 = 55
6 × 11 = 66
7 × 11 = 77
8 × 11 = 88
9 × 11 = 99
10 × 11 = 110
11 × 11 = 121
12 × 11 = 132

Twelve times table

1 × 12 = 12
2 × 12 = 24
3 × 12 = 36
4 × 12 = 48
5 × 12 = 60
6 × 12 = 72
7 × 12 = 84
8 × 12 = 96
9 × 12 = 108
10 × 12 = 120
11 × 12 = 132
12 × 12 = 144

Here is a multiplication grid showing all of the times tables up to the 12 times table.

This is how you use it.

To work out 7 × 9: with one finger go across from 7 and with another finger go down from 9. Where your fingers meet gives you the answer 63.

	1	2	3	4	5	6	7	8	9	10	11	12
1	1	2	3	4	5	6	7	8	9	10	11	12
2	2	4	6	8	10	12	14	16	18	20	22	24
3	3	6	9	12	15	18	21	24	27	30	33	36
4	4	8	12	16	20	24	28	32	36	40	44	48
5	5	10	15	20	25	30	35	40	45	50	55	60
6	6	12	18	24	30	36	42	48	54	60	66	72
7	7	14	21	28	35	42	49	56	63	70	77	84
8	8	16	24	32	40	48	56	64	72	80	88	96
9	9	18	27	36	45	54	63	72	81	90	99	108
10	10	20	30	40	50	60	70	80	90	100	110	120
11	11	22	33	44	55	66	77	88	99	110	121	132
12	12	24	36	48	60	72	84	96	108	120	132	144

 17 Use the grid to work out these tables facts:

6 × 8 = ☐

12 × 12 = ☐

9 × 7 = ☐

11 × 5 = ☐

8 × 12 = ☐

Congratulations on completing this practice book! Why not perfect those tables skills by moving on to the Easy Learning Times Tables Workbook?

Answers

Three times table

Page 4

15, 1, 3, 11, 9, 6, 3, 36, 9, 3, 24, 3

Page 5

Q1 6, 18, 30, 12, 15, 24, 33, 3, 21
Q2 3, 8, 1, 6

Four times table

Page 6

40, 4, 11, 8, 4, 16, 3, 4, 12, 32, 4, 7

Page 7

Q1 Double/double machine: 8, 16, 28

$\times$ 4 machine: 8, 16, 28

These number machines produce the same numbers.

Note to parent: your child should recognise that doubling a number twice is the same as multiplying a number by four.

Q2 16, 12, 24, 28, 32, 40, 36, 8, 4, 48

Mixed tables

Page 8

Q1 $2 \times 2p = 4p$; $6 \times 5p = 30p$; $6 \times 10p = 60p$
Q2 The numbers 10 and 20 have three different coloured rings around them.

The numbers 3 and 11 do not have any rings around them.

Note to parent: your child should recognise that the number 10 and 20 are answers in the 2, 5, and 10 times tables.

Page 9

Q3 $\times$ 2 / $\times$ 5 machine: 30, 50, 80

$\times$ 10 machine: 30, 50, 80

These number machines produce the same numbers.

Note to parent: your child should recognise that multiplying a number by 2 and then 5 is the same as multiplying a number by 10.

Q4 11×3; 7×4; 4×4; 8×3

Page 10

Q5 Colour red the shapes containing 4, 28, 32, 8, 40, 20, 16.

Colour blue the shapes containing 3, 6, 9, 18, 15, 21, 27, 30.

It's a skateboarder!

Q6 5 adult tickets £25; 7 adult tickets £35; 12 adult tickets £60

3 child tickets £9; 2 child tickets £6; 10 child tickets £30

You can buy 7 child tickets for £21.

Page 11

Q7 Shade in the letters c, r, e, p, a and s leaving the unshaded letters to spell the number thirty.
Q8 50, 8, 21, 16, 6, 9, 60, 9

Six times table

Page 12

30, 6, 6, 11, 12, 3, 6, 1, 6, 24, 6, 72

Page 13

Q1 24, 36, 54, 60, 12, 18, 42, 6, 30, 48
Q2 Shade in the letters s, i, n, r, a, m leaving the unshaded letters to spell the number twelve; twelve is the product of 2 and 6.

Page 14

Q3 Match: 4×6 with 24; 9×6 with 54; 3×6 with 18; 10×6 with 60; 2×6 with 12 and 7×6 with 42
Q4 36, 3, 1, 54, 11

Page 15

Q5 £18, £24, £72, £6, £48
Q6 $5 \times 6 = 30$; $6 \times 6 = 36$; $7 \times 6 = 42$; $4 \times 6 = 24$; $2 \times 6 = 12$

Seven times table

Page 16

7, 11, 56, 28, 5, 7, 84, 3, 7, 7, 14, 1

Eight times table

Nine times table

Eleven times table

Twelve times table

Q2 $4 \times 12 = 50$ ✗ $7 \times 12 = 84$ ✓
$5 \times 12 = 60$ ✓ $2 \times 12 = 22$ ✗
$10 \times 12 = 110$ ✗ $8 \times 12 = 98$ ✗
$12 \times 12 = 144$ ✓ $6 \times 12 = 74$ ✗

Page 34

Q3 $4 \times 12 = 48$ eggs; $7 \times 12 = 84$ eggs;
$3 \times 12 = 36$ eggs

Q4 24, 60, 84; 108, 72, 48

Page 35

Q5 36, 72, 24, 12, 84, 96, 48, 132; lime, plum, pear, apple. They are all fruits.

Q6 4 belts £48; 10 belts £120; 7 belts £84; 12 belts £144

Mixed tables

Page 36

Q1 $\times 8, \times 9, \times 11, \times 7$

Q2 **1** 42; **2** 7; **3** 66; **4** 5; **5** 4

Page 37

Q3 **1** 36; **2** 64; **3** 48; **4** 81; **5** 14; **6** 42; **7** 25; **8** 54; **9** 45; **10** 56; **11** 63; **12** 32; **13** 27; **14** 72; **15** 20

Q4 48, 42, 36, 30, 24, 18, 12
14, 28, 42, 56
72, 64, 48, 40, 32, 16
18, 27, 45, 54, 72, 81
120, 108, 96, 72, 48

Page 38

Q5 56 *Note to parent: Your child should recognise that the number 56 is an answer in the seven and eight times tables.*

Q6 3 multi-monsters: 9 heads, 18 eyes, 27 ears, 12 arms; 10 multi-monsters: 30 heads, 60 eyes, 90 ears, 40 arms; 7 multi-monsters: 21 heads, 42 eyes, 63 ears, 28 arms

Page 39

Q7 $6 \times 2 = 12$; $9 \times 3 = 27$; $8 \times 10 = 80$; $7 \times 3 = 21$; $6 \times 10 = 60$

Q8 $4 \times 11 = 44$; $8 \times 9 = 72$; $6 \times 9 = 54$; $12 \times 12 = 144$; $9 \times 12 = 108$; $5 \times 11 = 55$

Page 40

Q9 2 skateboards £18; 5 pencils 35p; 6 books £72; 8 yo-yos 80p; 4 footballs £44; 10 rubbers 40p; 7 trains £42; 9 badges 72p; 7 pencils; 6 trains; 5 books

Q10 $3 \times 6 = 18$; $4 \times 7 = 28$; $5 \times 8 = 40$; $2 \times 9 = 18$; $3 \times 10 = 30$; $4 \times 4 = 16$; $7 \times 6 = 42$; $6 \times 8 = 48$; $9 \times 7 = 63$; $8 \times 8 = 64$; $7 \times 12 = 84$; $10 \times 9 = 90$; $5 \times 4 = 20$; $9 \times 3 = 27$, $11 \times 11 = 121$

Page 41

Q11 Follow the path through 42, 21, 35, 30, 56, 63, 70, 24, 54, 7, 28

Q12 48, 6, 108; 48, 6, 108; both machines give the same answers.

Page 42

Q13 2×12 − red; 5×11 − white; 6×6 − brown; 4×9 − brown; 7×5 − pink; 8×6 − yellow; 5×4 − orange; 4×12 − yellow; 2×10 − orange; 6×8 − yellow; 4×6 − red

Q14 $72 − 8 \times 9$; $63 − 7 \times 9$; $45 − 9 \times 5$; $81 − 9 \times 9$

Page 43

Q15

x	1	2	3	4	5	6	7	8	9	10	11	12
1	1	2	3	4	5	6	7	8	9	10	11	12
2	2	4	6	8	10	12	14	16	18	20	22	24
3	3	6	9	12	15	18	21	24	27	30	33	36
4	4	8	12	16	20	24	28	32	36	40	44	48
5	5	10	15	20	25	30	35	40	45	50	55	60
6	6	12	18	24	30	36	42	48	54	60	66	72
7	7	14	21	28	35	42	49	56	63	70	77	84
8	8	16	24	32	40	48	56	64	72	80	88	96
9	9	18	27	36	45	54	63	72	81	90	99	108
10	10	20	30	40	50	60	70	80	90	100	110	120
11	11	22	33	44	55	66	77	88	99	110	121	132
12	12	24	36	48	60	72	84	96	108	120	132	144

Q16 ALMOST FINISHED!

Page 45

Q17 $6 \times 8 = 48$; $12 \times 12 = 144$; $9 \times 7 = 63$; $11 \times 5 = 55$; $8 \times 12 = 96$